Brother and Sister

Written by Chris Lutrario
Illustrated by Jeffrey Reid

Collins *Educational*
An imprint of HarperCollins*Publishers*

Paul was big. Pauline was little.

Paul liked to keep dry. Pauline liked to get wet.

Paul jumped down. Pauline climbed up.

Pauline wanted to go upstairs.

Paul wanted to go downstairs.

Paul stayed awake. Pauline fell asleep.

Paul was quiet. Pauline was noisy.

But they were both very hungry!